Angels

Understanding, Recognizing, and Receiving their Assistance Using Oracle Cards

Amanda J Evans

Copyright © 2020 Amanda J Evans

All rights reserved.

This paperback edition contains material protected under International and Federal Copyright Laws and Treaties. Any unauthorized reprint or use of this material is prohibited. No part of this book may be reproduced or transmitted in any form by any means, electronic or mechanical, including photocopying, recording, or by any information storage and retrieval system without express written permission from the author/publisher.

ISBN: 9798640873375

DEDICATION

For all those searching for a deeper meaning in life

CONTENTS

	Introduction	i
1	What are Angels?	1
2	What are Angel Card Readings?	Pg 16
3	Angel Cards Explained	Pg 18
4	Preparing to use your Angel Cards	Pg 21
5	Grounding and Protection Exercises	Pg 24
6	Reading your Angel Cards	Pg 29
7	Angel Card Spreads	Pg 32
8	Colors in Angel Cards	Pg 38
9	Symbols in Angel Cards	Pg 40
10	Putting everything into practice	Pg 48

INTRODUCTION

Angel card readings can be really accurate and give you some comforting guidance just when you need it the most. We all have within us the capability to read the cards. The most important thing that we can do is, believe in ourselves and our ability to communicate with the Angels.

Throughout this book you will find information on how to connect and communicate with your Angels through the use of Angel Cards. You will also discover how to read the cards for yourself and others and what spread to use for certain situations.

This is a very comprehensive book covering all aspects. It includes information on various Angel Card Spreads, colors and your cards, archetypes and more.

1 WHAT ARE ANGELS?

Angels are vibrations of energy that act as messengers of the Divine. They are messengers from the higher realms that allow us to have a great understanding and connection to spirit. The word angel comes from angelos which is the Greek word for messenger.

Angels are not just messengers; they are also part of your consciousness where they represent the realms beyond thought and idea. Throughout history angels have inspired poets, writers, artists, prophets and of course today, everyday men and women are delivering messages from the angels. There are references to angels in various religious texts such as the Koran, Bible and Torah. Angels have appeared in the art of the early centuries and have been integral to many of the religious stories we have grown up hearing about.

Angels are beings of light and love and they emerge from

purity of consciousness. They can teach us to have joy, laughter, peace, happiness, share kindness and appreciate beauty. They are here to heal us, guide us, assist us, and above all, lead us to connect with your creator self within.

Angels can of course become so much more and as you connect with and work with your angels you will come to understand exactly what I mean. Angels can give you guidance on all aspects of your life and help steer you in the right direction.

Angels can't tell you what to do or interfere in your life.

You were given free will and in order for the angels to work alongside you, you have to ask. The angels can never intervene in your life unless your life is in danger and it is not your time to cross over. We have all heard stories of people who say they have been saved from death by angels. This is because it wasn't their time to die and our guardian angels are allowed to intervene in such circumstances.

To connect with your angels is very easy. All you have to do is say out loud or mentally "Angels please come close and help me with ...."

We all have a guardian angel who has been with us since birth and who never leaves our side. Angel cards are a fantastic tool for building a stronger connection to your guardian angel. They can also help you to discover what you came to Earth to do. I use my angel cards every day to guide me and provide me with insight on what I should focus on for that day. This also helps to keep my connections strong and you too will see this happening the more you use them. It may seem a little daunting at first, but trust in the process and you will soon see the results.

The Archangels

There are different levels in the angelic realms and I'm sure many of you have heard of the Archangels. The Archangels are the overseers of the Angelic Realm. They work by the creator's side and in concert with the guardian angels to help humanity in powerful ways. Each of the Archangels has a specific job and they are available to everyone at all times. As with all angels, Archangels are not bound by time or space and can be with many people simultaneously. You simply need to ask for their presence and assistance and they will be there.

When you call upon the Archangels, you are bringing in strong, powerful energies that will create miracles in your life.

The names, rankings and meanings associated with the Archangels vary according to different religions and cultures and the exact number of Archangels also differs. The following list brings together most of the commonly known Archangels, all of whom are non-denominational. The Archangels offer their help to every person regardless of his or her belief system and they can be with everyone on the planet at the same time. You can call on any or all of the archangels to help you with any circumstance.

Archangel Michael:

Archangel Michael is one of the Archangels that I work most closely with. He usually brings with him a lot of warmth and I usually sense a blue color. He is the Archangel who oversees lightworkers and helps them unfold and fulfil their purposes. He helps with the release and transmutation of fear and negative energy. Call on Michael when you are feeling afraid in any way. He can help you feel safe and bring you the courage you need to move forward towards your desired goals. Michael also assists in cleansing negative energies from any person, place or thing. Michael is the Archangel that is called upon for the cutting on the cords, for protection and for courage. I always call upon Michael to watch over my family, friends and loved ones and to watch over anyone who may need protecting at this time. Michael is also great for helping when I am feeling afraid or lacking courage. I ask him to walk with me and stay with me every time I visit the dentist, go for an interview or any other situation where I may need a little bit of courage. Within minutes of calling on his I usually feel very comfortable and confident. There are a number of prayers that you can use to call on Archangel Michael. I usually just say, Archangel Michael be with me now and help me with ....

I have included two prayers below that you can use or you can make up your own. It really doesn't matter once your intention is there.

ANGELS – UNDERSTANDING, RECOGNIZING, AND RECEIVING THEIR ASSISTANCE USING ORACLE CARDS

"I now call upon the mighty and powerful Archangel Michael to stand with me. Please grant me the strength, courage, integrity and protection I need to fulfil my purpose in life. Please use your sword of light to cut away any doubts and negativity. Surround me with your blue cloak of protection so that I may always work on the side of good. Thank you."

Michael's energy is always very warm and you may feel the temperature of your room increasing when you call upon him.

Another wonderful prayer that you can use with Archangel Michael and a great one to use each morning is:

"Dear Lord Archangel Michael,
I call to you and your legions this day to wrap me in the blue veil of your protection. Let it descend upon me like a mantel and be sealed and held by the grip of Mother Goddess Earth, Sourced by Her white-fire core, Protecting me from all but the highest levels of light of Mother-Father God, From all non-Christed sources, from all evil and darkness, from all astral entities and energies, and from all other negatives – planetary, interplanetary, and universal, on-planet and off-planet, above and below me, to my left and to my right, in front and behind me, on this and all planes of existence, in this and all levels of consciousness, in this and all dimensions of time, known or unknown, now and forever.
Amen"
Louix Dor Dempriey

Archangel Gabriel

Archangel Gabriel can come in on either a male or female vibration. Known as the angel that announced the birth of Christ, Gabriel is associated with communication. You can call on Archangel Gabriel to assist you with any kind of communication, whether it is talking openly with a loved one or speaking your truth. Gabriel also assists writers, journalists and artists in getting their messages out to the world. I like to call on Gabriel whenever I sit down to write. I find that he helps the words to flow a little better and provides me with inspiration. Again you can call on Gabriel anyway you want but I have included a little prayer below to give you some ideas.

"I now invoke the mighty and powerful Archangel Gabriel to stand with me. Please bring me insights so that I may always walk in the light. Remove all my doubts and fears and purify my body, mind and spirit. Thank you"

Archangel Raphael

Archangel Raphael is the healing angel. Raphael works closely with those in healing professions and assists people in discovering their healing abilities. You can call on Raphael when you are physically ill or injured and you can also send him to be with anyone who is in need of healing. Archangel Raphael brings with him a beautiful emerald green colour and you may experience warmth or a coolness. He is very gentle and I use him all the time to help with healing and bringing comfort.

You can call on Archangel Raphael by using the prayer below:

"I now invoke the mighty and powerful Archangel Raphael to stand with me (or name). Please fill me (or name) with wholeness and good health. Help me (or name) heal the wounds from the past. Please heal and restore every aspect of my (or name's) being. Thank you."

Archangel Uriel

Archangel Uriel is an angel of wisdom. Again this angel can come in on a male or female vibration depending on exactly what energy you need at the time. This is the archangel who sheds light on darkness and is especially useful when you are feeling depressed, angry, victimised or confused. When you call on Archangel Uriel he will come with beautiful golden light that will help you to release emotions such as anger, unforgiveness and other negative emotions that may be preventing you from seeing clearly. Uriel is the angel to call upon to help you find peace and the answers you seek.

You can call on Archangel Uriel by using the prayer below:

"I now invoke the wise and powerful Archangel Uriel to stand with me (or name). Please fill me (or name) with your golden light. Help me (or name) to release the negative emotions that are clouding my judgement and preventing me from findings peace and answers. Thank you."

Archangel Ariel

Archangel Ariel is known as the angel of the Earth. This is

because this archangel works on behalf of the planets and oversees the elemental kingdom helping with the healing of all animals. Archangel Ariel's name means "lion or lioness of God". You can call upon Archangel Ariel to help you to make connections with the elemental kingdom especially the fairies. Archangel Ariel can also help you with environmental issues and to heal injured or sick animals.

You can call on Archangel Ariel by using the prayer below:

"I now invoke the mighty and powerful Archangel Ariel to stand with me (or name). Please help me (or name) to connect with the elemental kingdom and the energy of the fairies. Please help to strengthen my awareness and my ability to communicate with the fairies. Thank you."

This prayer can be adjusted depending on the reason you need to work with Archangel Ariel.

Archangel Azrael

Archangel Azrael's name means "whom God helps". Archangel Azrael is most commonly known as the "Angel of Death" because he is the angel who meets people at the time of their death and helps them to cross over to the other side. He helps those who have just died to feel comfortable and loved. Archangel Azrael also helps spiritual teachers and ministers of all religions. You can call upon Archangel Azrael to help your deceased or dying loved ones. He can also help with your spiritual teaching and help you communicate your message with more love and clarity.

You can call on Archangel Azrael by using the prayer below:

"I now invoke the mighty and powerful Archangel Azrael to stand with (name). Please fill (name) with comfort and love and help to make their transition into the spirit world a painless experience. Help them to realise how much they are loved and please help to bring peace and comfort to their loved ones who remain in physical form. Thank you."

This prayer can be adjusted if you are calling on Azrael for help with your spiritual teaching.

Archangel Chamuel

Archangel chamuel has many names including Camael, Camiel, Camium, Johoel, Seraphiel and Shemuel. His name means "he who sees God". Archangel Chamuel can help you to find important parts in your life. You can call on Chamuel to help you to find new love, new friends, a new job and even lost items. Once found, Archangel Chamuel can help you to build and maintain these new situations. Chamuel works on the pink ray which is the vibration of love and you can call on Chamuel if you need help in sorting out any misunderstandings in any of your personal or work relationships.

You can call on Archangel Chamuel by using the prayer below:

"I now invoke the loving and powerful Archangel Chamuel to stand with me (or name). Please help me (or name) to find that which is missing in my life. Help me (or name) remove the obstacles and blocks that prevent me from finding that which I seek. Please heal all misunderstandings and fill my life with love. Thank you."

Archangel Haniel

Archangel Haniel's name means "grace of God" and normally comes forward on a female vibration. You can call on Haniel whenever you want to add things such as grace, peace, serenity, enjoyment of good friends' company, beauty and harmony to your life. You can also call upon Archangel Haniel before any event where you feel you might need grace such as giving an important presentation, being interviewed for a job, going on a first date and more.

You can call on Archangel Haniel by using the prayer below:

"I now invoke the loving and graceful Archangel Haniel to stand with me (or name). Please fill me (or name) with grace (whatever you need). Thank you."

Archangel Jeremiel

Archangel Jeremiel is the archangel who inspires and motivates us to devote ourselves to spiritual acts of service. His name means "mercy of God" and he is also involved in the process of attaining divine wisdom. You can call on Archangel Jeremiel if you feel stuck spiritually and you want to regain your enthusiasm about your spiritual path and divine mission.

You can call on Archangel Jeremiel by using the prayer below:

"I now invoke the loving and wise Archangel Jeremiel to stand with me (or name). Please fill me (or name) with your loving wisdom and help me to find the enthusiasm that is missing in my life. Help me (or name) remove the obstacles and blocks that prevent me from finding that which I seek. Thank you."

Archangel Jophiel

Archangel Jophiel's name means "beauty of God" and she is the patron archangel of artists. She helps us to see and maintain beauty in life. You can call on Archangel Jophiel before you being any artistic project. Archangel Jophiel is also involved in beautifying the planet by cleansing it of pollution so you can call on Jophiel for help in clearing clutter from your home or in any environmental clearing you may be taking part in.

You can call on Archangel Jophiel by using the prayer below:

"I now invoke the beautiful and powerful Archangel Jophiel to stand with me (or name). Please help me (or name) to find the beauty that is missing in my life. Help me (or name) remove the obstacles and blocks that prevent me from seeing that which I seek. Thank you."

Archangel Metatron

Archangel Metatron's name means "angel of presence" and he is one of the two archangels whose names don't end in "el". It is thought that Archangel Metatron once walked upon the earth as the prophet Enoch. Metatron works with Mother Mary to help children both living and crossed over. You can call on Archangel Metatron for any kind of assistance you may need with your children. His intervention often involves helping children open their spiritual awareness and understanding. Archangel Metatron also works with sacred geometry.

You can call on Archangel Metatron by using the prayer below:

"I now invoke the loving and powerful Archangel Metatron to stand with me (or name). Please help me with my children and give me the patience and understanding I need. Thank you."

Archangel Raguel

Archangel Raguel's name means "friend of God" and he is often called the Archangel of justice and fairness. You can call on Raguel whenever you feel that you are being overpowered or manipulated. Archangel Raguel will intervene by giving you guidance about how to attain balanced power and fairness within the structure of your personal and community relationships. You can also call on Archangel Raguel on behalf of another person who is being unfairly treated.

You can call on Archangel Raguel by using the prayer below:

"I now invoke the loving and powerful Archangel Raguel to stand with me (or name). Please help me (or name) to find justice and balance. Thank you."

Archangel Raziel

Archangel Raziel's name means "secret of God". Archangel Raziel is said to stand very close to God so that he hears all the divine conversations about universal secrets and mysteries. It is said that Archangel Raziel wrote these secrets into a document that he gave to Adam, which eventually ended up in the hands of the prophets Enoch and Samuel. You can call on Archangel Raziel whenever you need help understanding esoteric material or to engage in alchemy or manifestation.

You can call on Archangel Raziel by using the prayer below:

"I now invoke the loving and powerful Archangel Raziel to stand with me (or name). Please help me (or name) to understand what I need to know now. Thank you."

Archangel Sandalphon

Archangel Sandalphon's name means "brother" and he is the twin brother of Archangel Metatron. Archangel Sandalphon is the Archangel of music and prayer. He assists Archangel Michael in clearing away fear and the effects of fear using his gift of music. You can put on soothing music and call on Archangel Sandalphon to remove any fear or confusion you may have.

You can call on Archangel Sandalphon by using the prayer below:

"I now invoke the loving and powerful Archangel Sandalphon to stand with me (or name). Please fill me (or name) with your beautiful music. Help me (or name) remove the obstacles and blocks that prevent me from finding the answers and understanding I seek. Thank you."

Archangel Zadkiel

Archangel Zadkiel's name means "righteousness of God". Zadkiel helps us to attain freedom through forgiveness and he is known as the patron archangel of those who forgive. You can call upon Archangel Zadkiel to help you release anger and the effects that anger and un-forgiveness can cause. Archangel Zadkiel helps us to view others with compassion instead of judgment.

You can call on Archangel Zadkiel by using the prayer below:

"I now invoke the loving and forgiving Archangel Zadkiel to stand

with me (or name). Please fill me (or name) with understanding and the power to forgive and release myself from the effects of anger. Thank you."

When it comes to the Archangels there is a lot more information available. You may find that different books and people provide different information and characteristics for each Archangel but you will find that the main traits remain the same.

2 WHAT ARE ANGEL CARD READINGS?

Angel card readings refer to the ability of a person, through the use of cards, to receive and convey messages from the angels. With angel card readings a person uses angelic oracle cards to provide guidance and give answers to those who come for a reading. These readings can involve the past, present and future of the person. Angel card readings also include direct communication with the angels at all times. Angel card readings always provide positive messages and there are no negative messages in any communication with the angels.

During an angel card reading the reader connects with the angels using the cards as a communication tool. The cards that they pull relate to the information and messages that the angels wish the person having the reading to receive. These messages can be based on a specific spread or questions that the person has asked in advance.

ANGELS – UNDERSTANDING, RECOGNIZING, AND
RECEIVING THEIR ASSISTANCE USING ORACLE CARDS

Why People Go For Angel Card Readings

There are several reasons why people go for angel card readings. Most of the time, they use them for guidance with their career paths, relationships, health, wealth, past life issues and life purpose. When a person finds themselves caught at a crossroads and they need to make major life decisions, the guidance from the angels can really help. Our human eyes cannot see all things and getting help from our guardian angels can help us to see things much clearer. Many people may have an idea of what they need to do and require an acknowledgement that what they are planning will bring them the happiness they desire. This is why many people are drawn to the messages the angels bring because they are always positive and uplifting.

Who Can Do Angel Card Readings?

Anyone can do angel card reading. It really is just a matter of connecting with your angels. Some people find it easy to tap into their psychic ability while for some it takes a lot more practice.

3 ANGEL CARDS EXPLAINED

Many people today feel drawn to working with their Angels and Guides especially after a spiritual experience. When you look through a deck of angel cards you will find that they contain a small positive message, a simple phrase or a couple of words. Interpreting what these messages mean is a matter of practice and trust on your part. All angel card decks will come with a small booklet that will explain the meaning behind each card but your focus should be on receiving the meaning of each card from your own angels rather than depending on the booklet. The booklet is just a guideline and your own intuition should be used to give messages. Using angel cards is a great way to build your relationship with the angels.

Types of Angel Card Decks

There are numerous different types of angel card decks available by various angel card authors. Some names that might be familiar to you include Doreen Virtue, Diana

Cooper, Colette Baron Reid and more. These decks can be bought in book shops, new age, spiritual shops and online from websites such as Amazon. Some of these decks are called oracle cards and others work with specific archangels such as the Archangel Michael and Archangel Raphael cards. As a beginner, I found that Doreen Virtues cards were the easiest to work with, but once I progressed, I found that I really like Colette Baron Reid's cards, especially the artwork that comes with these. I still use these cards today in many of my readings as well as the Archangel Michael cards by Doreen Virtue.

Choosing Your Angel Cards

You should always choose angel cards that you are naturally drawn to. These are ones that your intuition tells you are right for you. If you are buying them from a local shop you can ask if there are any open decks that you can look at. If you are buying them online you should be able to view images on the cards and it also helps to read the testimonials from others who have used the cards. You may have seen cards belonging to your friends or family.

It may be helpful to spend some time looking at the different angel card decks that are available and then see which ones seem to stand out for you. It is important that you feel comfortable with your choice especially when choosing your first deck.

Getting To Know Your Angel Cards

Once you have your cards the next step is getting to know them and attuning them to your energy. It is important to take some time getting to know your angel cards. Take some quite time for yourself when you first open them. Hold them close to your heart and ask your angels to bless them and help you to read the cards accurately. Next take the time to go through each card, touching everyone in turn so that you infuse them with your energy. Spend some time playing with your cards, reading them, shuffling them, fanning them out and perhaps spreading them out on a table. All of these things will energize your cards and tune them into your own unique vibration. In doing this you will be able to connect to your cards using both your conscious and your subconscious.

A good way to become familiar with your cards is to pick a card each day. You might want to mentally ask your angels what you need to know today and then choose a card from the deck. Read the message and them remember it throughout the day. Doing this on a daily basis is a great way to familiarize yourself with your cards and learn the meaning behind each one.

4 PREPARING TO USE YOUR ANGEL CARDS

You should always keep your cards clean and in a safe place. They are sacred and it is important that you treat them this way. You can place your cards in a velvet bag or in a special box if you have one. It is important to clear and cleanse your cards after every use. You should also cleanse your cards before you use them. This is to ensure that any energies that were picked up from the emotions of a previous reading or from the environment they were in such as the shop where you bought them are cleansed away to ensure a clear and accurate reading.

Cleansing Your Angel Cards

There are a number of ways to cleanse and clear your angel cards and these are things that you should familiarize yourself with if you want clear and accurate readings from your cards.

Drawing your deck through the smoke of a smudge stick or sage is a traditional method when it comes to cleansing and clearing cards. You can also use incense such as Frankincense which is perfect for connecting with the angelic realms. Again you just have to place the cards in the smoke.

Placing an amethyst on top of your deck can help to keep the energies pure.

Visualizing a white light penetrating and cleansing your cards is a beautiful way to clean them.

Lightly tapping on the top of your cards three times whilst holding the intention of freeing all old energies and releasing them from the deck is another way to cleanse your cards.

Cleansing Your Aura/Room/Home

Sage sticks often called smudge sticks are great for cleansing. They give off a thick smoke when they are lit and this smoke has powerful cleansing properties. Waft the smoke over your aura to cleanse it. You can also use this to clear negative energies in your room or home by wafting the smoke into the entire room paying particular attention to all the corners of the room. Open the windows and let all the energies to escape and fresh air to come into the room. This is an excellent technique to use when preparing your room for an angel card reading.

Using Candles

Candles have been used for centuries in rituals and magic.

ANGELS – UNDERSTANDING, RECOGNIZING, AND RECEIVING THEIR ASSISTANCE USING ORACLE CARDS

Lighting a candle while you do your spiritual work or card readings signifies bringing in "the light", or the higher realms. You can blow out your candle at the end of the session to bring your reading to an end.

5 GROUNDING AND PROTECTION EXERCISES

Grounding and protection is paramount in any spiritual work and it is something that you should do on a daily basis. Before any card reading you need to ground yourself and then protect your energy.

Grounding

The first thing you need to do when grounding is to place yourself in a relaxed position. Close your eyes and release the tension in your muscles. Take a deep breath and focus your breathing for a few moments. The next thing you need to do is visualise or imagine a beam of white light coming from above and entering your head through your crown chakra. This white light fills the upper part of your head and then moves down to the third eye chakra and then through the rest of your head, down through the throat chakra. The light continues to move down along your spine, down your shoulders and arms, your heart chakra and your chest. The light moves further down to your stomach and through your internal organs, down your whole body right the way down to your feet. This white light fills your entire body. While the white light is filling up your body, negative emotions and beliefs about ourselves, and problems/emotions of others that we have absorbed in our energy system are driven out. You should allow your breath to follow the cleansing white light supporting the removal of negative energies. You should allow yourself to continue to feel the white light going up and down your body cleansing and clearing all negative energy. You may feel the energy as warmth or tingling along your spine or you might not feel anything at all. After you have cleansed your energy it is now time to ground yourself. You begin to focus on your feet. See or feel roots growing from the soles of your feet into mother earth. See them anchoring you to the centre of the earth. Feel the attachment to the earth and then begin to draw the energy from the earth up into your body, energising and grounding you. You can then bring the earth energy up as far as your heart chakra and allow it to meet the white light here. Ask Archangel Michael to come in and seal the two energies together to keep you grounded during your work. Grounding helps to keep you feeling peaceful and centred.

Protection Techniques

Protection is used to help keep unwanted negativity and spirits out of your energy field. It is important to use protection if you are doing any type of spiritual work because you will be opening yourself up to contact with other realms. If you are sensitive to absorbing other people's emotions, difficulties, negative thoughts or even physical pain, it is really important that you pay particular attention to protecting yourself. If you sense that others may be tapping into your energy or sending negative energy your way then you can immediately put a shield of protection around yourself. It is important to protect yourself from anything that can lower your vibration.

Using A Mirrored Ball

The mirrored ball technique is a very powerful protection technique. It is great to use if you feel like you are under psychic attack or if you are going somewhere where there is a lot of healing taking place. It is very simple to do. Visualise a mirrored disco ball, step inside it and see it completely seal you. Any negative energy that comes your way will be reflected back to where it came from. The additional bonus to using this technique is that any negative energy that touches the mirrored ball is immediately transmuted and completely healed meaning that love is sent back to the owner to help with their healing.

Coloured Light

Coloured light is another great protection method. You visualise a column of light coming down from the higher realms. See this light form a sphere around you sealing you inside. You can layer different colours for additional protection if you want.

Pink light is used to protect you from negative minded people. If you are around people who are gossiping or complaining, pink light will keep these energies away from you as only love can penetrate this light.

Purple light is great for psychic protection. It protects against psychic attack and entities.

Green light is a physical healing shield. Put it around yourself or someone else who is in the process of healing.

White light invokes additional angels to surround you. It is helpful against physical attack and crime against your belongings.

Lead Shield

Using a lead shield is another very powerful technique that can be used in protection. Use this whenever heavy duty protection is required. This could be on entering a nasty conflict with someone. You should visualise yourself completely surrounded from all angles with a lead shield. Nothing can penetrate this shield.

Archangel Michael

Archangel Michael is the main angel to call on for protection. You can ask him to keep you protected and to shield you from any energies that are not for your highest good. You can call on Archangel Michael at any time.

Prayers For Protection

Morning Prayer

I ask, and it is my intent to surround myself in a seamless bubble of the Christ White Light, to protect me now, forevermore, and always, and to only allow that Energy that is for my soul's highest and best good to come through. So be it, it is done. Thank you.

Evening Prayer

I ask, and it is my intent to remove, release, detach, and I command any and all excess unnecessary toxic and unhealthy energy to exit out of my body and I send it to the Christ White Light. So be it, it is done. Thank you.

Prayer For The Angels of Healing And Protection

May the angels bless me with divine protection. May the healing love of the angels surround me wherever I go. I ask that I may be a vehicle for spiritual healing. I ask that I may receive angelic healing on a daily basis. My spirit is constantly healing by ministering angels. My guardian angels always guide me to the healers, doctors and therapists that can best help me. I thank my angels for their transformative influence upon my soul. I ask that I may learn to heal myself, become more positive and evolve spiritually. I ask that I may bless the lives of others with the healing and protection of the angels.

6 READING YOUR ANGEL CARDS

When it comes to angel card readings there are several methods to choose from. They are all equally effective and accurate. Everyone has a different way of reading and it is important that you find the one that you are most comfortable with. It is perfectly fine to develop your own style other than the ones shown in this manual.

The first thing you have to do is your preparation which is listed in the previous pages. Then still your mind, hold your cards and ask the Angels to communicate with you through the cards.

If you are doing a reading for yourself, simply ask your angels to either answer your question or to tell you what they want you to know by guiding you to the relevant cards. If you are reading for someone else you ask your angels to help you to communicate what the person you are reading for needs to know.

Method 1

Shuffle the cards while mentally or verbally asking the angles a question. You will feel, hear, see or know when to stop shuffling. Fan the cards out in front of you and place them face down. Ask the angels how many cards you need to choose for the person and be aware of the answer you receive. Run your hand over the cards and intuitively pick your first card, you may feel a tingle or heat or just know which one to pick. Place the first card to your left with the picture side up. Choose your next card in the same way and place this to the right of the first card. Continue doing this until you have chosen all your cards.

The first card you have chosen will represent the immediate past. The next represents the present and the next represents the future. Each card after the third represents future events, usually in increments of one to three months. It is important to understand though that circumstances change as our thoughts, attitudes and outlooks change.

*****Jumping cards are essentially important. These cards are the ones that the angels would like you to pay particular attention to.***

*****Upside down cards indicate that there is a resistance or blockage in that area.***

Once you have chosen all your cards the next step is to study the message on each card. It is important that you trust your intuition when reading your messages. Your first instincts will usually be the right ones. This is where trust and practice really comes into play. The more you

ANGELS – UNDERSTANDING, RECOGNIZING, AND RECEIVING THEIR ASSISTANCE USING ORACLE CARDS

practice the better your guidance will become and the more open you will be to receiving the messages from your angels. When reading your cards try to see them as a story and you are telling the story using the cards. The first card tells the person what has brought them to where they are in the present moment and you use this to continue telling your story by the way the remaining cards relate.

It is important that you always follow your instincts first. Each card will have many different meanings and even those which are not included in the booklet that accompanied your cards. If you pick a card that says LOVE for example and you feel that the person needs to GIVE love then you must say so. If you feel the card means that their angel or guide is SENDING love, then say so. Do not spend time worrying about getting it wrong, your cards are your tools that allow you to connect with the angels and you will never get cards that don't make sense if you are genuinely working with the light.

Always remember to say "thank-you" to your angels after every reading you do.

In the next section of this book we are going to look at the different angel card spreads that you can use in your readings.

7 ANGEL CARD SPREADS

Usually when reading cards, you lay them out in spreads (patterns on the table). With a little research you can find lots of different spreads in books but it is worth noting that there really is no right or wrong way to work with your cards. When using spreads, each card represents a question or part of an answer and the layout of the cards will help you to remember which card is for which question. Below you will find information on some of the more popular spreads that you can use with your angel cards readings. As you become more familiar with your cards and more comfortable with doing readings you may come up with your own spreads.

With all the spreads it is about practice and of course trusting that the angels will provide you with the cards you need to give the best reading. You need to trust that you are connected with the angels and allow them to bring the messages to you. You need to let your intuition do most of the work and if you feel or sense something just say it without second guessing the information you are getting.

Asking Specific Questions

Most people who come for angel card readings want to know about either love, money or work situations. You can easily work with a single question. As with tarot cards, it is better to use at least three cards but you can use as many as you need to answer the question.

Angel Message Of The Day (One Card Spread)

This spread is used to ask the question "what do the angels want me to know today?" It might not make sense at that moment but be sure to keep it in mind because before the end of the day you will know why. This spread is a great way to practice and get to know your angel cards. You can choose a different card every day. This spread is also useful if you require specific answers such as "what will happen if I do X?"

Guardian Angel Spread (three card spread)

This spread can be used to answer the questions where have I been? Where am I now? Where am I going?

Card 1 relates to the past and shows past experiences, the ones that cast a light on the current situation.
Card 2 relates to the present and this card reveals what you are feeling and experiencing at the moment.

Card 3 relates to the future and predicts the results of the course of action that you will take based on the first two cards.

Three card spreads are always used to answer past, present and future questions, such as what is coming up for me? Will my life get better soon? For more information you can use six cards placing an additional card under each of your three cards. These additional cards will give more specific information on the first cards.

Soulmate Spread (four card spread)

For questions such as: "Is [Name of person] my soulmate?", "How does this person feel about me?" or "Where is this relationship headed?"

Card one shows the purpose of the relationship.
Card two shows the blocks in the relationship.
Card three gives you the angels guidance.
Card four shows the probable outcome based on current circumstances.

What The Angels Want Me To Know Spread (four card spread)

For questions such as "I would love to receive a message from my Guardian Angel (or deceased loved one)" or "Who are my Guardian Angels or Spirit Guides?"

Card one is the general theme of the day, situation, or

relationship.
Card two shows the possible block.
Card three is the Angels guidance to heal this block.
Card four is the probable outcome, based on current thoughts and circumstances.

Archangel Card Spread (five card spread)

This spread can be used to answer questions such as What should I do?

Card one relates to the present or general theme of the reading.
Card two represents past influences that are still having an effect.
Card three shows the future.
Card four shows the reason behind the question (this will probably shed light on card 2) and a blockage which is stopping you from achieving your desired result.
Card five shows the potential within the situation and the possible results from taking a given course of action.

New Love Spread (five card spread)

For questions such as: "When will I meet my soulmate?" or "How will I meet my soulmate?"

Card one shows how to prepare to meet the new person.
Card two shows the other person's blocks.
Card three shows your blocks.

Card four shows the Angels guidance to heal these blocks.
Card five represents the Angels message about this new relationship.

Life Purpose Spread (five card spread)

For questions such as: "What is my life purpose?" or "What steps should I take in my career?" or "Is this new business idea a good idea?"

Card one shows what you have learned in the past.
Card two shows what you are currently learning.
Card three shows what steps to take right now.
Card four shows how you can best help others.
Card five shows your life purpose.

Spirit Family Reading (seven card spread)

You can use this spread to invoke the power and wisdom of all your angels to guide you on your journey.

Card one represents the challenge.
Card two shows the influences from the past.
Card three shows what you need to do.
Card four shows what you are working on.
Card five shows what you need to know
Card six show the new opportunities on the way.
Card seven shows the best course of action.

Yearly Spread

With this spread you are asking the angels for guidance for the coming year starting from the next month to come. The first card is taken from the top of the deck and placed to your left. The next card is then placed to the right and this continues until you have twelve cards. Each of the cards represents monthly increments. As you progress using this spread you can add an additional card or two for each month which will give you more information such as what the beginning of the month brings, the middle of the month and the end of the month.

Asking Specific Questions

Most people who come for angel card readings want to know about either love, money or work situations. You can easily work with a single question. As with tarot cards, it is better to use at least three cards but you can use as many as you need to answer the question.

8 COLORS IN ANGEL CARDS

Colors can give you a lot of different information when reading angel cards. Colors have their own spiritual meanings and when you understand these, the angels can use them to provide you with even more guidance. In this section we will cover the different colors and what they can mean. When reading cards, you may find that certain colors stand out or catch your attention. If you understand what these colors mean it will give you more insight into what your reading is about.

Colors will generally have two meanings depending on whether they are dark or light.

White: purity, joy, truth, peace, enlightenment, neutrality.

Black: Death, power, emptiness and sorrow. It is the color of the night and may refer to things that are hidden. It is also the color of renewal and transformation.

Blue: Feelings, the unconscious, intuition, unity, harmony, reflection and tranquility. It can also represent coldness, depression and mourning.

Green: Fertility, growth, abundance, nature, wealth, money and youth. It is the color of spring and may refer to a new beginning. Green is also the color of healing.

Orange: Ambition, action, forcefulness, energy, enthusiasm, security and balance.

Purple: The color of royalty. It represents justice, nobility, mystery, pride and envy. It is also the color of spirituality.

Yellow: The color of illumination. It represents joy, happiness, optimism, intelligence. It may also represent weakness, cowardice and fear.

Gold: The color of the universe and sun. It represents realization, success and spiritual learning.

Silver: Mystery, contemplation, hidden wisdom, femininity and intuition.

Gray: Sadness, mourning, emotional turbulence, humility, old age and dullness.

9 SYMBOLS IN ANGEL CARDS

Symbols can also help when reading angel cards. Certain elements can provide even more information for your readings. In this section we will cover different animals and elements and what they can mean in a reading.

Animals in card readings

Animals can reflect our instinctive natures. They can expose our primal needs, desires and behaviours. In card readings animals can offer an insight into our characters, often shedding light on how our natures and behaviours are influencing a situation.

Birds: Birds are associated with thoughts and spiritual aspirations. Birds in flight represent freedom from limitation.

Bulls: Bulls are associated with power, fertility, charging ahead and generosity. They can also be associated with stubbornness and denial.

Butterflies: Butterflies are the image of transformation and may indicate a change of thought, change of action or change of circumstance.

Crab: Crabs are unique because they have mastered the ability to escape by moving sideways. They can also be defensive and overprotective. They can move through water and this means they have the tools to move through their emotions.

Dog: Dogs are faithful companions and they represent loyalty and protection. Dogs can also represent the need to have trust and may signify the arrival of a new helper.

Dragon: Dragons represent the use of our intelligence. They symbolise protection and security. The shedding of their skin can represent a transformation of some kind.

Eagle: Eagles are the bridge between heaven and earth. In a reading they can signify the need to look for hidden spiritual truths. Eagles can also represent creativity, healing, freedom and the need for courage.

Fish: Fish live in water and usually represent the emotional world. Fish can represent the subconscious, the dream world, creativity and prosperity.

Horse: The horse represents travel and personal power. When a horse appears in a reading it means movement. An action might be required. Horses can also symbolise work and can mean more work coming in.

Lion: The lion rules the heart and represents the need for courage in the face of apprehension. The lion may also indicate the need to release stress. The lion is a leader and enjoys seeing his supporters achieve success.

Snake: The snake represents transitions or transformations in one's life journey. The snake may also represent fertility, the need for a more masculine approach to a situation, and can identify the areas in our life where we may need to adjust or adapt.

Landscape Imagery In Card Readings

Now that you understand the animals and colours in card readings let us look at the landscape imagery. This is the background imagery and it is an important element in cards that often gets overlooked. Understanding the meanings of these can help to deepen your readings.

Clouds: Clouds represent thoughts, ideas, divine messages and intervention. Clouds can also indicate confusion and lack of clarity.

Fields: New opportunities, the beginning of a new endeavour, fertile ground, creative efforts and hard work. Fields may also indicate the fruition of your labour or actions.

Flowers: Birth, happiness, joy, friendship, giving and receiving. Flowers are also associated with the attainment of beauty.

Horizon: The horizon line typically indicates what is in consciousness and what remains in the unconscious.

Lightening: A moment of truth, divine intervention, being struck into consciousness. In a reading lightening may indicate the need to let go of old ideas.

Mountains: Obstacles, conflicts, life transitions, abstract thoughts. Mountains can indicate that there is a spiritual lesson that must be learned. Mountains also refer to the attainment of your goals.

Moon: Karma, fate, femininity, intuition. When there is a moon in your card reading it may suggest that you must move into a new level of awareness. The moon signifies the onset of a new phase in one's life.

Paths: The direction of your actions, the karmic journey, the distance it takes to complete a goal or assignment. Paths can also indicate beginnings and endings.

Rain: Detoxification, grief, tears, sombre meditation and the need for acceptance.

Rocks: Small obstacles, difficult relationships, unforeseen complications. In readings rocks may also denote the denial of a current circumstance or relationship.

Sea: The unconscious, the emotions, dreams, power, mystery, travel. The sea can refer to your emotional state within the context of a situation. The sea can also indicate when your emotions are ruling over everything else.

Snow: Cold, difficult, isolated, harsh conditions and a time to do nothing.

Stars: Guidance, a new direction, a time to shine, coming into your own.

Sun: Development, growth, happiness, joy, realisation, enlightenment, illumination. In a reading the sun may also indicate a positive foreshadowing of an event to come.

Water: That which is felt and not seen, relationships, love, emotions, the flow of things, mystery and depth.

Waterfall: Water is a symbol of emotion and the subconscious. Therefore, waterfalls deal with the constant running and flowing movement of our emotions and the stirring movements of our deeper minds. Observing the nature of waterfalls, we see they typically move at such a rushing speed that they tend to take everything with them in their path. In card readings this means that we mustn't let our emotions run away from us. The waterfall plummets down dropping and crashing and this is a lesson that when we are not in control of our emotions and thoughts they control us and can lead to our demise.

Other Signs and Symbols

Arches: Stability, support, new beginnings, gateways. In a reading arches can indicate transitions and they often reflect new opportunities.

Bench: The bench is symbolic of taking a moment to examine the details. In a reading benches indicate the need to sit back, relax and take some time to examine the situation.

Blindfold: Focus on the inner world. Blindfolds can refer to one's inability to look at reality.

Boat: Travel, a passage and a change in direction. Boats are associated with water so they can also signify a time for reflection on your feelings prior to making a life change.

Bridges: The link between two worlds. Bridges also refer to character strengths such as your ability to overcome obstacles with the use of your skills.

Castle: Obtaining your desires, being on the right path, the fruits of your labour. In card readings castles can indicate the need to solidify the foundation of our ideas. It is from these foundations that we can manifest our desires.

Chains: Restriction, being tied to a situation, lack of freedom, bondage and the addiction to the material.

Children: Regeneration, promise, hope and innocence. Children can represent the need to find the child within yourself. They can also signify the need to alter your perception and look at the world from new eyes.

Cross: Union between the male and female energies, union with a higher power and balance.

Fire: Passion, power, destruction and creativity.

Fountain: Peace, abundance and harmony.

Hammer: Hard work is required but you possess the necessary skills. If a hammer comes up in a reading it may be the need to communicate your opinions and thoughts more clearly.

Horn: The horn is a symbol of announcement. They symbolise a joyous, boisterous, victorious, triumphant announcement. They signal that something has happened or is about to happen soon. They can announce both victory and attack.

House: One's concept of self, safety, secrets and protection.

Keys: Opened, closed, locked, imprisoned and freed. Keys refer to all that we block and all that we unlock. They are associated with knowledge and can refer to liberation through wisdom.

Lantern: Search for truth, enlightenment, the presence of the divine in a difficult time, self exploration and the journey of self discovery.

Pitcher: The things that you hold dear to you. Purity, nourishment, transformation and sustenance.

Scales: Balance and equality. Scales can refer to where one is ignoring certain aspects of their life that require attention.

Shield: Guarded, protection, hidden aspects of ourselves. The shield often informs us where we need to restrain from our overindulgences.

Tower: False ideas, shaky foundations and apprehension.

Wheel: Cycles, motion, travel, universal energy and creativity.

Wreath: Attainment, success, wisdom, victory and protection.

10 PUTTING EVERYTHING INTO PRACTICE

Now that you have all the information you need, the next thing is practice. I would recommend that you start by choosing a card of the day every day. Be aware of this card throughout the day and ask the angels to help you to understand the knowledge the card is giving you. If you get a card that say for example asks you to focus on joy and happiness, you must do your best to stay positive and look for experiences throughout the day that will bring you joy and happiness. For every one of these that you experience, remember to thank that angels for bringing this experience to you.

I would also recommend that you keep what I called an angel journal. In this you can write down what your card of the day was, what happened that day, what angel experiences you had, etc. Doing this will also strengthen your connection with the angels. The more you

ANGELS – UNDERSTANDING, RECOGNIZING, AND RECEIVING THEIR ASSISTANCE USING ORACLE CARDS

acknowledge their presence the more you will notice them in your life. You can ask the angels for help with so many things. I always ask for good parking spaces and I get them. I also ask for help to keep me motivated and focused on tasks that I want to complete. When my children are playing up, I ask the angels to come in and help to keep them calm and help me to keep calm too. It always works. You can try asking the angels for help within anything you can think of because the more you ask the more they will help. The only thing that you need to remember is to say thank you.

The angels will also give you signs that they are around if you ask them. You may begin to notice feathers or coins. You might also hear a specific song on the radio where the words answer a question you have been asking. Guidance can come in so many ways, but it is up to you to notice it.

MORE ON ANGELS

You can find out more about the angels and the messages that they wish the world to receive by reading Amanda J Evans's book "Messages From The Angelic Realms". This book is filled with inspirational and helpful messages and is a book that can be picked up and opened on any page. Whatever the situation just open this book for a profound and inspiring message from the angels. This book is available in both paperback and kindle format.

For a signed copy of this book, you can contact me directly via my website www.amandajevans.com

I hope you have enjoyed this ebook and found the information useful. I am always available to answer any questions that you might have. I appreciate you taking the time to read this book and humbly ask that you leave a review if you have the time.

Blessings,

Amanda
xxx

Printed in Poland
by Amazon Fulfillment
Poland Sp. z o.o., Wrocław